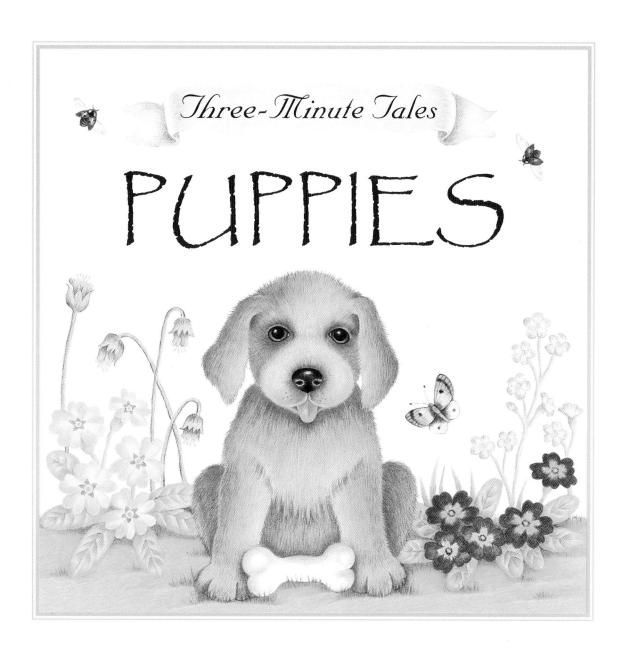

Three-Minute Tales

PUPPIES

p

This is a Parragon book
First Published in 2000

Parragon
Queen Street House, 4 Queen Street,
Bath, BA1 1HE, UK

Produced by The Templar Company plc
Pippbrook Mill, London Road, Dorking,
Surrey, RH4 1JE, UK

Designed by Kilnwood Graphics

Printed and bound in Spain
ISBN 0 75253 608 7

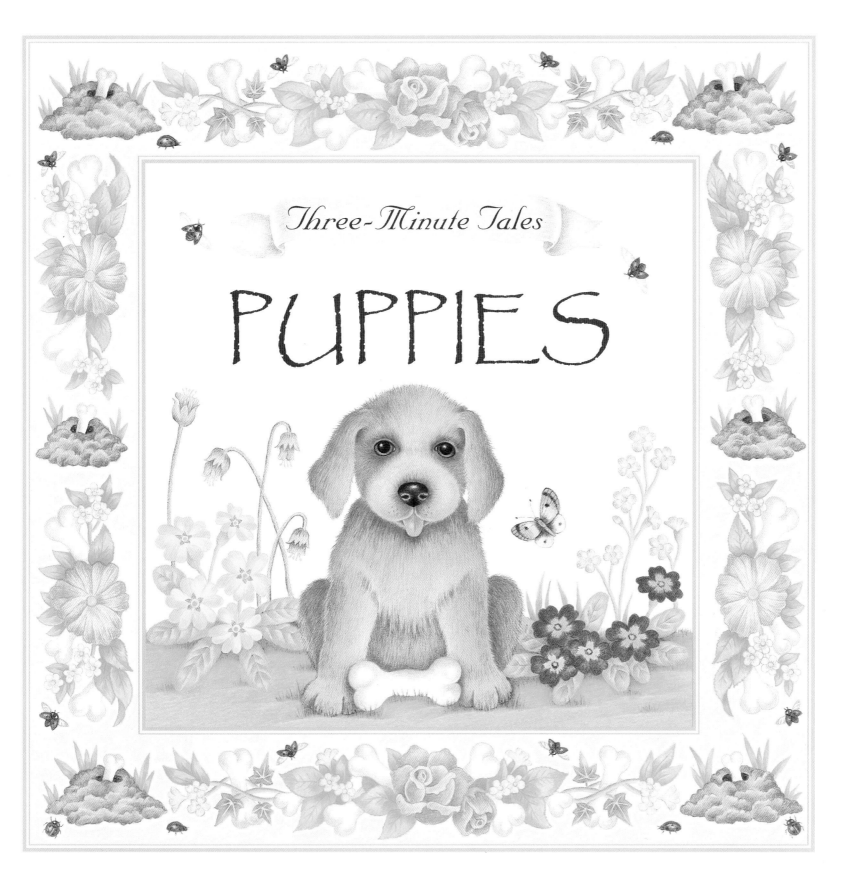

Three-Minute Tales

PUPPIES

Written by Caroline Repchuk • Illustrated by Stephanie Boey

CONTENTS

Chasing Tails

Bone Crazy!

ONE STORMY NIGHT

It was Patch's first night outside in his smart
new kennel. He snuggled down on his warm
blanket and watched as the skies grew dark.

Before long he fell fast asleep.

As he slept, big spots of rain began to fall.

A splash of water dripped from the kennel
roof on to his nose, which started to twitch.

Just then, there was a great crash and a bright flash of light lit up the sky. Patch woke with a start and was on his feet at once, growling and snarling. "It's just a silly old storm," he told himself.

"Nothing to scare a fearless farm dog like me!"
But as the lightning flashed again, he saw a
great shadow looming against the barn.
Patch gulped. Whatever could it be?

Patch peered into the darkness, but could see nothing through the rain. Just then, the sky lit up once more, and sure enough, there was the shadow, but larger and closer than before! Patch began to bark furiously, trying to act braver than he felt. Next time the lightning flashed, there was no sign of the shadow. "I soon scared that monster away!" he thought.

But as Patch settled back down in his cosy
kennel, the sky outside lit up once more,
and there in the doorway towered the monster!
"Just checking you're okay in the storm," said

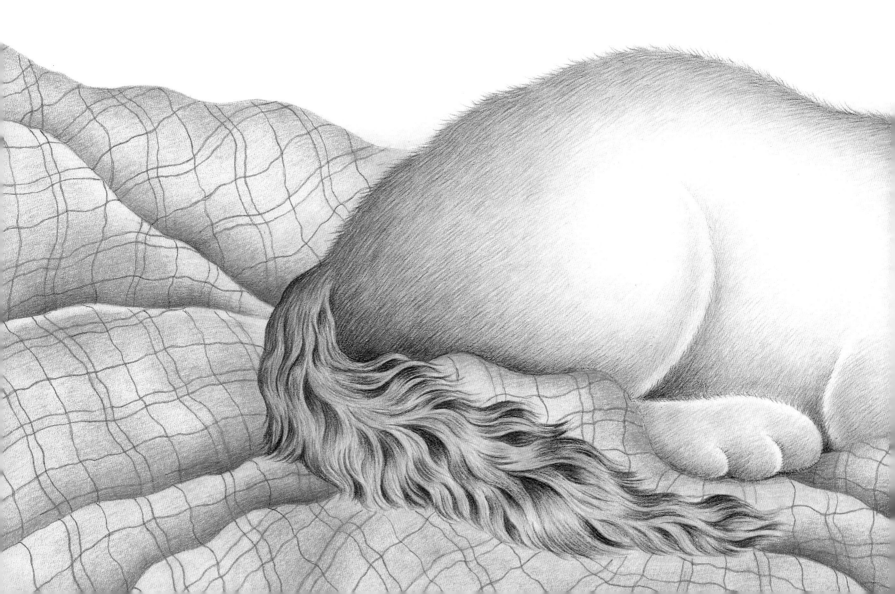

Mummy, giving Patch a gentle lick on the ear.
"A fearless farm dog like me?" said Patch.
"Of course I am!" But as the storm raged
on, he snuggled up close to her all the same!

SMELLY PUP

All the animals were gathered in the barn.

"It has come to our attention," said Mrs

Hen to Smelly Pup, "that you are in need

of a bath. You haven't had one all summer.

Even the pigs are complaining!"

Smelly Pup just laughed. "Me? Take a bath?

That'll be the day!" he said, and off he went.

Outside Smelly Pup strolled through the
farmyard, muttering, "What a crazy idea.
I'm a dog. I do dog things… like chasing cats!"
The farm cat leapt up hissing as Smelly Pup

came racing towards her. He chased her all around the farmyard. Then, just as he was about to catch up, she sprang into the air. Smelly Pup took a great leap after her...

... and landed in the pond with a SPLASH!
"Silly Pup!" smirked the cat from a nearby tree.
The ducks quacked as he spluttered and
splashed, chasing them through the shallows!
The water felt cool and refreshing on his fur.
After a while, he came out and rolled on the
nice muddy bank. "That was fun," he said.
"Maybe I could get used to baths after all!"

CHASING TAILS

Barney had been chasing his tail all
morning. Round and round he went, until he
made himself feel quite dizzy.
"Can't you find something useful to do?"
asked the cat, from where she sat watching
him on the fence.
"What? Like chasing lazy cats?" said Barney,
as he leapt towards her, barking fiercely.

Later, as he trotted around the farmyard,
Barney thought about what the cat had said.
He wished he could be more useful, but he
was only a little pup. When he grew up,
he would be a fine, useful farm dog, like his mum.

Just then, he rounded the barn, and there
in front of him waved a big bushy tail...
"Here's a tail I can catch!" thought Barney
playfully, and he sprang forward and sank
his sharp little puppy teeth into it!

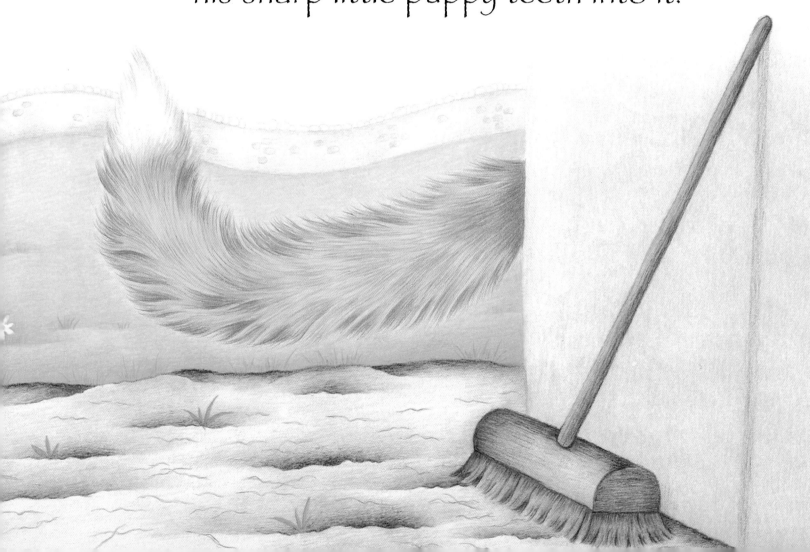

Now, the tail belonged to a sly fox, who was
about to pounce on Mrs Hen and her
chicks! The fox yelped in surprise, and ran
away across the fields.

"Ooh, Barney, you saved us!" cried Mrs Hen.

The cat was watching from the fence.

"Maybe all that practice chasing tails has
come in useful after all!" she said.

BONE CRAZY!

Alfie sat in his basket chewing on a large
bone. Mmm! It tasted good. When he had
chewed it for long enough, he took it down to
the bottom of the garden, to bury it in his
favourite spot, beneath the old oak tree.
He didn't see next door's dog, Ferdy,
watching him through a hole in the fence.

The next day, when Alfie went to dig up his
bone, it was gone! He dug all around, but it
was nowhere to be found. Just then, he spied
a trail of muddy paw prints leading to the
fence, and he realised what had happened.

Alfie was too big to fit through the fence and get his bone back, so he thought of a plan, instead! Next day he buried another bone. This time, he knew Ferdy was watching him.

Later he hid and watched as Ferdy crept into the garden and started to dig up the bone. Just then, Ferdy yelped in pain. The bone had bitten his nose! He flew across the garden and through the fence leaving the bone behind. Alfie's friend Mole crept out from where the bone was buried. How the two friends laughed at their trick! And from then, Ferdy always kept safely to his side of the fence!

The End